THE WORLD FOLKTALE LIBRARY

Tales from Hispanic Lands

Tales from Hispanic Lands

Selected by Lila Green

Illustrated by Donald Silverstein

Consultants

Moritz A. Jagendorf
Author and Folklorist

Carolyn W. Field
Coordinator of Work with Children
The Free Library of Philadelphia

SILVER BURDETT COMPANY

Morristown, New Jersey
Glenview, Ill. • Palo Alto • Dallas • Atlanta

INTRODUCTION

Folktales are old. They are easy to remember, and fun to listen to and to tell. Most folktales are stories that were told and retold long before the invention of books and printing. That is how they got their names. They were passed along by word of mouth—one folk told another folk. Fathers told children. Neighbor shared with neighbor. Merchants told innkeepers. Innkeepers told visiting sailors and sea captains, who carried the stories to the far corners of the world. Sometimes words, names, and details were changed as the tales were passed along, but the ideas about life and people changed very little.

Folktales are not usually about real people or actual events, but in a way they are almost always true. They tell us something real about the people who pass them along. These folktales are from people in Spain and other Spanish-speaking lands in the Western Hemisphere. The stories express some of the values of these societies, and reveal their ideas about living and surviving. The stories are about the joys and hopes of a people, as well as about their worries and fears. Each story tells us a little about life as certain people see it.

Folktales may come from unfamiliar people and different parts of the world. But there is something in each one that you will recognize and understand. In this way, folktales show that people are very much alike the world over. You may recognize Juan Bobo, who is like Simple Simon. Or, you may be familiar with Señor Rooster, who takes on Señor Fox in a battle of wits. There's a story from Puerto Rico about a rabbit who was so clever that. . . . Well, if you are about to be eaten by a tiger, maybe you had better read about this rabbit right away!   THE EDITOR

Table of Contents

THE FLEA

Spaniards have a special love for friendly animals. Among their favorites are three who appear in this story: La Hormiguita, the ant; Ratonperez, the mouse, and El Escarabajo, the beetle.

Once there was and was not a King of Spain. He loved to laugh; he loved a good joke as well as any common person. Best of all, he loved a riddle.

One day he was being dressed by his chamberlain. As the royal doublet was slipped over the royal head, a flea jumped from a safe hiding-place in the stiff lace ruff. It landed directly upon the King's nose.

Quicker than half a wink, the King clapped his hand over the flea and began to laugh. "Por Dios, a flea! Who ever heard of a King of Spain having a flea? It is monstrous—it is delicious! We must not treat her lightly, this flea. You understand my

Lord Chamberlain, that having jumped on the royal person, she has now become a royal flea. Consider what we shall do with her."

But the chamberlain was a man of little wit. He could clothe the King's body but he could not add one ribbon or one button to the King's imagination. "I have it!" said the King at last, exploding again into laughter. "We will pasture out this flea—in a great cage—large enough for a goat—an ox—an elephant. She shall be fed enormously. When she is of a proper size I will have her killed and her skin made into a tambourine. The *Infanta*, my daughter, shall dance to it. We will make a fine riddle out of it. Whichever suitor that comes courting her who can answer the riddle shall marry with her. *There* is a royal joke worthy of a King! Eh, my Lord Chamberlain? And we will call the flea Felipa."

In his secret heart the chamberlain thought the King quite mad; but all he answered was: "Very good, Your Majesty," and went out to see that proper pasturage was provided for Felipa.

At the end of a fortnight the flea was as large as a rat. At the end of a month she was as large as a cat who might have eaten that rat. At the end

of a second month she was the size of a dog who might have chased that cat. At the end of three months she was the size of a calf.

The King ordered Felipa killed. The skin was stretched, dried, beaten until it was as soft, as fine, as silk. Then it was made into a tambourine, with brass clappers and ribbons— the finest in Spain.

The Infanta, whose name was Isabel, but who was called Belita for convenience, learned to dance with Felipa very prettily; and the King himself composed a rhyme to go with the riddle. Whenever a suitor came courting, the Infanta would dance and when she had finished, the King would recite:

"Belita—Felipa—they dance well together—
Belita—Felipa; now answer me whether
You know this Felipa—this animalita.
If you answer right, then you marry Belita."

Princes and dukes came from Spain and Portugal, France and Italy. They were not dull-witted like the chamberlain and they saw through the joke. The King was riddling about the tambourine. It was made from parchment and they knew perfectly well where parchment came from. So a prince would answer: "A goat, Your Majesty." And a duke would answer: "A sheep, Your Majesty"—each sure he was right. And the Infanta would run away laughing and the King would roar with delight and shout: "Wrong again!"

But after a while the King got tired of this sheep and goat business. He wanted the riddle guessed; he wanted the Infanta married. So he sent forth a command that the next suitor who failed to guess the riddle should be hung—and short work made of it, too.

That put a stop to the princes and dukes. But far up in the Castilian highlands a shepherd heard about it. He was young, but not very clever. He thought —it would be a fine thing for a shepherd to marry an Infanta, so he said to his younger brother: "Manuelito—you shall mind the sheep and goats; I will go to the King's palace."

But his mother said: "Son, you are a *tonto*. How should you guess a riddle when you cannot read or write, and those who can have failed? Stay at home and save yourself a hanging."

Having once made up his mind, nothing would stop him—not even fear. So his mother baked him a *tortilla* to carry with him, gave him her blessing and let him go.

He hadn't gone far when he was stopped by a little black ant. "*Señor* Pastor," she cried, "give me a ride to the King's court in your pocket."

"La Hormiguita, you cannot ride in my pocket. There is a tortilla there which I shall have for my breakfast. Your feet are dirty from walking, and you will tramp all over it."

"See, I will dust off my feet on the grass here and promise not to step once on the tortilla."

So the shepherd put the ant into his shepherd pouch and tramped on. Soon he encountered a black

beetle who said: "Señor Pastor—give me a ride to the King's court in your pocket."

"El Escarabajo, you cannot ride in my pouch. There is a tortilla there which I shall presently have for my breakfast—and who wants a black beetle tramping all over his breakfast!"

"I will fasten my claws into the side of your pouch and not go near the tortilla."

So the shepherd took up the beetle and carried him along. He hadn't gone far when he came up with a little gray mouse who cried: "Señor Pastor, give me a ride to the King's court in your pouch."

But the shepherd shook his head. "Ratonperez, you are too clumsy and I don't like the flavor of your breath. It will spoil my tortilla that I intend to have for my breakfast."

"Why not eat the tortilla now and then the breakfast will be over and done with," and Ratonperez said it so gently, so coaxingly, that the shepherd thought it was a splendid idea. He sat down and ate it. He gave a little crumb to La Hormiguita, a crumb to El Escarabajo and a big crumb to Ratonperez. Then he went on his road to the King's court carrying the three creatures with him in his pouch.

When he reached the King's palace he was frightened, frightened. He sat himself down under a cork tree to wait for his courage to grow.

"What are you waiting for?" called the ant, the beetle and Ratonperez all together.

"I go to answer a riddle. If I fail I shall be hanged. That isn't so pleasant. So I wait where I can enjoy being alive for a little moment longer."

"What is the riddle?"

"I have heard that it has to do with something called Felipa that dances, whoever she may be."

"Go on and we will help you. Hurry, hurry, it is hot in your pouch."

So the shepherd climbed the palace steps, asked for the King and said that he had come to answer the riddle.

The guard passed him on to the footman, saying, "*Pobrecito!*"

The footman passed him on to the lackey, saying, "Pobrecito!"

The lackey passed him on to the court chamberlain, saying, "Pobrecito!!" And it was his business to present him to the King.

The King shook his head when he saw the shepherd-staff in his hand and the shepherd-pouch hanging from his belt, and he said: "A shepherd's life is better than no life at all. Better go back to your flocks."

But the shepherd was as rich in stubborness as he was poor in learning. He insisted he must answer the riddle. So the Infanta came and danced with the

tambourine and the King laughed and said his rhyme:

"Belita—Felipa—they dance well together—
Belita—Felipa; now answer me whether
You know this Felipa—this animalita.
If you answer right, then you marry Belita."

The shepherd strode over and took the tambourine from the hand of the Infanta. He felt the skin carefully, carefully. To himself he said: "I know sheep and I know goats; and it isn't either."

"Can't you guess?" whispered the black beetle from his pouch.

"No," said the shepherd.

"Let me out," said the little ant; "perhaps I can tell you what it is." So the shepherd unfastened the pouch and La Hormiguita crawled out, unseen by the court. She crawled all over the tambourine and came back whispering, "You can't fool me. I'd know a flea anywhere, any size."

"Don't take all day," shouted the King. "Who is Felipa?"

"She's a flea," said the shepherd.

Then the court was in a flutter.

"I don't want to marry a shepherd," said the Infanta.

"You shan't," said the King.

"I'm the one to say 'shan't,' " said the shepherd.

"I will grant you any other favor," said the Infanta.

"I will grant you another," said the King.

"It was a long journey here, walking," said the shepherd. "I would like a cart to ride home in."

"And two oxen to draw it," whispered the black beetle.

"And two oxen to draw it," repeated the shepherd.

"You shall have them," said the King.

"And what shall I give you?" asked the Infanta.

"Tell her you want your pouch filled with gold," whispered Ratonperez.

"That's little enough," said the Infanta.

But while the royal groom was fetching the cart and oxen; and the lord of the exchequer was fetching a bag of gold; Ratonperez was gnawing a hole in the pouch. When they came to pour in the gold, it fell through as fast as water, so that all around the feet of the shepherd it rose like a shining yellow stream.

"That's a lot of gold," said the King at last.

"It's enough," said the shepherd. He took his cart, filled it with the gold and drove back to the highlands of Castile. He married a shepherd's daughter and there they lived without a care in the world. That's a happy life, you might say—for anyone who would choose it.

THE TIGER AND THE RABBIT

The Spaniards enjoy telling about tiny creatures who defeat mighty ones. In Spain, the little creature may be the mouse or the ant, but in Central America, it is often the rabbit. The rabbit was brought to the New World in the African stories of long ago. This story is told in Puerto Rico.

Long, long ago all the animals were friends and lived at peace with one another, except the Tiger. For the Tiger had promised himself to eat small animals, especially the Rabbit if he ever crossed his path.

But the Rabbit was very clever and known for his quick wit. He knew that the Tiger wanted to eat him, and though he considered the beast stupid, clumsy, and a fool, he managed to keep away from his path and thus avoid trouble. But this was not always possible, since both of them liked to roam about.

One day, when the Tiger was bringing home a coil of rope, he met the Rabbit resting under the shade of a tamarind tree. The Tiger dropped the rope and rushing to the Rabbit, said, "Aha! Today you shall not escape me. I will eat you up."

The little Rabbit was at once on the alert, but answered calmly: "You might as well. I have been trying to die, for if you knew what is going to happen, you wouldn't care to live, either. Eat me up and be done with it. But for you, ah! I am sorry—sorry."

Eager as the Tiger had been to eat the Rabbit, the fear of what was going to happen got the better of him, and the idea of saving himself was foremost in his mind. The Rabbit saw his confusion and waited patiently for the question he was sure would come.

"What is going to happen, Rabbit?" the Tiger asked.

"Why, haven't you heard?" answered the Rabbit. "A terrible hurricane is coming on, stronger than any one we have ever had."

Now, there was nothing the Tiger feared more than hurricanes. He shivered at the thought of the howling of the wind, the crashing of trees, and the downpour of rain.

"Oh, little Rabbit," he said, "what am I to do? You are so small that you can hide anywhere. You are so light on your legs that you can run miles away, but what about me? Help me, please."

The Rabbit remembered the rope the Tiger was carrying home, and looking up at the large tamarind tree under which he stood, a plan came to his mind.

"There is only one thing," he said, "only one thing to do. I must tie you to this tree. It has stood several hurricanes and will no doubt stand this one, too."

"Tie me quick," answered the Tiger.

So the Rabbit tied him with the coil of rope and firmly wound the rope around the thick trunk of the tamarind tree. Then he climbed up into the tree so that he could watch the Tiger.

Pretty soon a number of small goats passed by, and when they saw the Tiger stretched on the grass firmly tied to the tamarind tree, they bleated for joy.

"You wouldn't bleat so happily," said the Tiger, "if you knew what is going to happen."

"What?" asked the little goats, who, for the first time, found themselves speaking to the Tiger.

"A terrible hurricane is coming on, stronger than any one we have ever had," he said.

"Ha! Ha! Ha!" laughed the goats. "A hurricane indeed! We come from all up and down the mountain path, and from the green pastures on the hills, and

nowhere have we heard such news. There is no hurricane coming."

Gone were the Tiger's fears, and at once he noticed how fat the little goats were and what a tasteful morsel each one would make.

"Untie me, please," he pleaded.

But the little goats scampered away to tell the other animals that for once they could rejoice free of care, for the Tiger was tied firmly to a tamarind tree.

The Tiger wriggled and wriggled, and tried in vain to free himself. Up in the tree the little Rabbit was enjoying the sight below. Just then, a monkey swung down from a tree near-by. When he saw the Tiger, he let out a screech that brought down a large number of his friends.

"Untie me, please," pleaded the Tiger again.

"If we do, you will eat us up," answered the monkeys.

But the Tiger promised not to eat them up, and the monkeys began to work at the ropes. They gnawed at the knots until, little by little, they finished the work and set him free. No sooner done, the Tiger turned upon them, clawing and biting the poor monkeys, who, taken by surprise, began to jump screeching with all their might. Some ran wildly through the forest, while others climbed the near-by trees. All but one escaped, and the Tiger now turned fiercely upon him.

Just then, the Rabbit called down:

"Tiger, that is not the way one eats a monkey. I certainly wouldn't do it that way."

"How would you do it?" he called back.

"Ah, I would throw the monkey up and catch it in my mouth," answered the Rabbit.

"That is easy enough," said the Tiger.

So he threw the monkey up into the air, but his aim was so poor that he threw him right on the branches of a tree. He stood with his mouth wide open, waiting for the monkey to drop.

The Rabbit then shook a branch of the tamarind tree, and down dropped a large number of tamarind pods, right into the Tiger's mouth.

Poor Tiger, half choking and shaking his head to free his mouth of the fruit, ran through the forest,

vowing more than ever that he would eat up the
Rabbit the very next time he met him.

Time passed, and for a long time the Rabbit
avoided the Tiger. One morning, when he was sitting
on a rock near the lagoon, a peasant rode up on his

horse. He was on his way to market, the saddlebags filled with guava paste and fresh goat's cheese. The Rabbit noticed that the leaves covering the saddlebags were parched and dry. He could smell the fresh cheese, and his mouth watered as he thought of the round, delicate morsels, neatly wrapped up in leaves, resting at the bottom of the bags. Coming near the stone where the Rabbit sat, the peasant stopped his horse.

"Market is a long way yet," said the Rabbit. "Already the leaves covering your cheese are dry. I know some nice green leaves which will hold the moisture until you reach the market. They will help keep the cheese fresh and cool. I will bring you some leaves if you let me have two of your cheeses."

Now the peasant had been riding for a long time, and the sun had been hot. It was cool by the lagoon. He looked at the saddlebags and noticed also how the sun had dried out the leaves covering his merchandise. So he agreed to the Rabbit's offer.

Off scampered the Rabbit, away into the woods, and was soon back with tender green leaves, which the peasant was glad to have in exchange for two cheeses.

After a while, he was gone, leaving the Rabbit with his treasure. The Rabbit had not been eating long, when who should appear but the Tiger.

"Aha!" he cried. "Today, I will eat you up."

"Of course you will," answered the Rabbit, "but first, do have a taste of this delicious cheese."

"It is wonderful," said the Tiger. "Where did you get it?"

"Oh," answered the Rabbit, "from the bottom of the lagoon. See, I have another one here." And he showed him the other remaining cheese, which he had carefully wrapped up in leaves.

"How did you get them?" asked the Tiger, forgetting his threat to eat up the Rabbit.

"I tied two stones on my legs and jumped into the lagoon. It is full of cheeses."

"Then I will do the same," said the Tiger, looking around for some stones large enough for him.

"Well, I'll be running along," said the Rabbit. "Please leave some of the cheeses for me. I will take another dive tomorrow," and he left, chuckling to himself.

The Tiger tied four large stones to his legs and jumped into the water.

"Gulp, gulp." He swallowed mouthfuls of water as he sank deeper and deeper. He looked around carefully, but nowhere did he see the delicious cheeses which the Rabbit said were there. He realized then that the Rabbit had fooled him again. He felt the current pulling him. It carried him down and finally threw him onto a place full of branches and cattails.

"Help, help!" he cried, but no one heard him. He tugged at one of the branches. It was firmly rooted and he was able to pull himself up. He shook his big

head and sat down to let the sun dry his fur.

"I will eat up that Rabbit," he said to himself, "the very next time I see him."

For days he looked for the Rabbit, but could not find him anywhere.

Long after this adventure with the Tiger, the Rabbit paid a visit to his friend the Fox, and the conversation fell on the subject of the Tiger. The Fox was a great admirer of the Tiger and thought he was very clever and intelligent. He said the Tiger could do anything he wanted; nothing ever stood

in his way. The Rabbit, who knew better, began to laugh.

"He is a fool, that's what he is," he said. "A big fool. Why, he is such a fool that he lets himself be used as a horse by his friends."

"I don't believe it," said the Fox.

"I will prove it to you," answered the Rabbit, "and when I do, I hope you will be at your door to answer my greeting."

Time went on and the Fox forgot the Rabbit's foolish talk. One Sunday, he decided to invite some of his friends for a feast. He prepared special things to eat, but was discouraged because he had not been able to get music for entertainment. Just then the Tiger arrived, and wishing to help him, offered to bring the best guitarist he could find. It so happened that the Rabbit was the best guitarist in the place and the only one available, so the Tiger decided to look him up. He came to Rabbit's door and knocked.

"Who is there?" asked the Rabbit.

"It's the Tiger. I have come to get you to play at the Fox's feast."

"Go away," answered the Rabbit. "I am sick and cannot go."

"But you must come," said the Tiger. "There is no one to play and I have promised the music."

"Aha!" thought the Rabbit. "This is my chance."

"If you come," said the Tiger, "I won't ever try to eat you up—I promise."

The Rabbit wrapped a handkerchief around his head and, leaning on a cane, opened the door.

"I cannot walk, as you well see," he said.

"I will carry you on my back," offered the Tiger, who did not want to disappoint his friend, the Fox.

The Rabbit climbed on his back, but no sooner did he climb when he slid down again.

"Oh! Oh!" he cried. "I can't sit on your back unless I have a blanket. Now I have a little one here. . . ."

"All right," said the Tiger, "put it on my back."

After that the Rabbit climbed on again, but no sooner was he on, when down tumbled the blanket and the Rabbit with it.

"Oh! Oh!" he cried again. "I can't sit on a blanket unless I have a saddle. Now I have a little one here. . . ."

"All right, all right!" said the Tiger. "Bring it out, but only hurry, hurry."

Along with the saddle came a bridle and a pair of spurs. When the Rabbit finished harnessing the Tiger, he limped into his house again and came out with his small guitar. Pretending he was very sick, he took some time to climb on the Tiger's back, groaning feebly.

"Let us go, Tiger," he said at last, picking up the reins.

On trotted the Tiger, and pretty soon they came into view of the Fox's home. The Rabbit quickly cast off the handkerchief from his head and set the spurs to the Tiger's flanks. Up went the Tiger's legs; he reared like a horse, and sped along past trees and shrubs and finally past the Fox's house.

"*Adiós!* Good-by, Fox!" called the Rabbit, as he sped by.

Great was the Fox's surprise as he recognized the Rabbit on the Tiger's back. Like a flash, the Rabbit's promise came to his mind. The Rabbit was correct.

"The Tiger is a fool, a great fool," said the Fox.

By that time the Rabbit had come back and now stood at his door, laughing—and the Tiger followed him.

"Fox," Rabbit called, "I did prove it to you! Didn't I?"

That day, he played better than ever . . . . And now the Tiger, realizing how clever the Rabbit was, before the feast ended, they became the best of friends.

THE HOLES OF LAGOS

In many countries, people tell of a make-believe town—a foolish town, full of foolish people. In Finland, for example, the town is Holmola. In Poland, it is Chelm. And in Mexico, it is Lagos.

"Lagos! Where is Lagos?"

"Far, far away."

"How far?"

"As far as far can be in Mexico."

"How far is that?"

"Well . . . . I can't tell exactly."

"What part of Mexico?"

"I can't tell. Maybe any part of Mexico. Some people say one place; some say another; but, wherever that town is, it is full of foolish people."

"Aren't there foolish people everywhere?"

"Yes, but in Lagos *every* man is a *bobo.* The

Reprinted by permission of the publisher, The Vanguard Press, from *The King of the Mountains: A Treasury of Latin-American Folk Stories*, by M. A. Jagendorf and R. S. Boggs. Copyright © 1960 by M. A. Jagendorf and R. S. Boggs.

people of Lagos are different from those of any other town in Mexico. Everywhere there are *some* fools; but in Lagos they are *all* fools."

"That can't be."

"Oh, yes it can! In Lagos they do things people would do nowhere else. Take, for example, the time they found a deep hole in the center of the plaza, not far from the church."

"What happened?"

"Well, this is what happened."

One morning the mayor of the town was walking in his bare feet across the plaza, on his way to the city hall. When he got near the church, he discovered a deep hole, big enough for three men to fall into. He stopped and looked at the hole for a long time.

"How did this hole come to be in the plaza of Lagos?" he cried. "Who put it there?"

When no one answered, he called to the town policeman, who had a big torn *sombrero* on his head and a thin stick in his hand.

"How did that hole get there?" cried the mayor.

"I don't know, *Señor* Alcalde."

"If you, the guardian of peace in Lagos, do not

know, then nobody knows."

"That is true, Señor Alcalde."

"It's dangerous to have a hole like that in our town plaza. If people walk to church or to the city hall, they might fall into it and get hurt."

"Quite true, Señor Alcalde."

"Well, then, it must be closed at once."

"That's right, Señor Alcalde."

"Get the men of Lagos immediately and have them fill up that hole."

"*Sí*, Señor Alcalde."

The mayor went into the city hall to attend to business, and the policeman went to assemble all the men of Lagos who were sitting on their heels. And there were plenty of these. They took shovels and began digging up the earth from a place nearby and threw it into the hole. When the sun sank behind the hill, the hole was filled and the earth over it was smooth as a leaf. Everyone was satisfied with the day's work and went home to eat *tortillas*.

Later, when the mayor came out of the city hall, the policeman said politely:

"Señor Alcalde, you see that the hole is filled. The men did a fine job."

"I'm glad to hear it. We have good men in our town, better than any in Mexico."

"Thank you, Señor Alcalde. *Buenas tardes.*"

"Buenas tardes."

The mayor walked away. He hadn't walked far until he came to a second hole, the one from which the earth had been taken to fill the first hole. He stopped and looked at it in surprise.

"Another hole!" he exclaimed. "How did *this* hole get here? I didn't see it this morning. . . Carlos! Carlos!" he shouted.

The policeman came running.

"Yes, Señor Alcalde."

"There is a hole here. Look!"

"Yes, Señor Alcalde, there is," said Carlos, looking at it.

"People going to church or to the city hall could fall into it and break a leg, or even a neck."

"Well they might, Señor Alcalde; they certainly might."

"It must be closed at once, Carlos."

"Yes, it must be closed at once, Señor Alcalde," agreed Carlos, taking off his sombrero and scratching his head, "but the men have all gone home to eat their tortillas and go to bed. Everybody will be sleeping now."

"That's true," said the mayor. "Then *mañana*."

"Tomorrow it will be done, Señor Alcalde."

Early next morning Carlos had the men of Lagos digging up the earth not far from the new hole.

The mayor passed by on the way to his office, watched the men at work, and smiled in satisfaction.

"There are no workmen in all Mexico better than the workmen of Lagos," he said aloud, and went to the city hall.

The men all heard what he said and were pleased, and they continued their work with greater zeal. Soon the second hole was filled and the earth smoothed down.

At the setting of the sun, the mayor came by and saw the hole filled and the ground over it as smooth as a church floor.

"Carlos, that is good work."

"The men of Lagos are good workers, Señor Alcalde," agreed Carlos.

The mayor walked on; but he hadn't walked far when he came to a new hole.

"*Por Dios!* Holes grow in Lagos like weeds in a corn patch. How did this hole come to be here? Carlos! Carlos!"

Carlos came running.

"What's happened, Señor Alcalde?"

"There's another hole here in the ground. Look!"

Carlos looked. "Yes, Señor Alcalde, there is another hole in the ground."

"It must be filled."

"Yes, it must be filled, Señor Alcalde."

"People crossing the plaza might fall into it and break a leg."

"They might indeed break a leg, Señor Alcalde," said Carlos.

"Fill it at once."

Carlos removed his sombrero and scratched his head.

"The men have gone home to eat their tortillas, and soon they'll be asleep."

"True," said the mayor, ". . . quite true. Well then, mañana."

"Yes, Señor Alcalde."

Next morning, bright and early, the good men of Lagos were out digging again. From a spot nearby they dug up earth and filled the hole. When the sun set it was done.

The mayor passed by on his way home.

"This is good work, indeed," he said when he saw the hole filled, smooth as glass. "What excellent workers these men of Lagos are! There are none finer in all Mexico."

"That's true, Señor Alcalde," Carlos agreed.

The mayor continued on his way, and soon came to a new hole.

"Por Dios," he cried, "a new hole! There is a curse of holes on our town. Some evil spirit has wished them on us. Carlos! Carlos!"

Carlos came running.

"There is a new hole. See!"

"So there is, Señor Alcalde."

"It must be filled. At once."

"But the men will be asleep."

"Then mañana, Carlos."

This went on and on. Everyone in Lagos tried to figure out how it happened and why there were so many holes in their town, but they couldn't. They were just that kind of people.

So they kept on filling holes by digging new holes until they came to the edge of town.

Now, the people of the next town had been watching the work of Lagos day by day, laughing and saying nothing. But when the hole was next to their own town, they filled it with things lying around that they had been wanting to bury for a long time.

When the mayor of Lagos saw the last hole filled, and could not find another, he was very happy and said, "The men of Lagos never give up a job until it is finished."

The men of Lagos were happy, too, for they said

they were getting a little tired of so much digging
every day.

So everyone was happy, and there were no more
holes in Lagos.

SENOR BILLY GOAT

One of the helpful Spanish creatures appears again in this gentle story from Puerto Rico.

Once there was and was not, up in the Highlands in Puerto Rico, a little old woman and a little old man. They were very happy and lived contented in their peasant hut thatched with straw. Together they shared a vegetable garden in which they grew peppers, tomatoes, radishes, turnips, pumpkins, potatoes, beans, and corn. They spent hours talking over their garden, and the savory dishes they would prepare with some of the vegetables, and planning what they would do with the money they would receive from the vegetables they would sell at the market.

In the morning while his wife was busy brewing the coffee, the husband would rush to the window,

From *The Tiger and the Rabbit and Other Tales* by Pura Belpré. Copyright © 1978 by Pura Belpré. Copyright 1944, 1946, 1965 by Pura Belpré. Published by Eliseo Torres.

and say, "*Ay*, Maria! my darling. What beauty! Look at my lettuce. There is nothing in the garden like it."

That would bring María running to the window, and she would say, "Ay, Ramón! Put on your glasses and see for yourself, for it is blind, blind as a bat you must be. Look at my corn and my radishes! Such glowing colors! What gold! What red! Fit for a king's mantle!"

And then both would laugh at each other and turn back to enjoy the hot coffee which María had left on the table.

Now, one morning, when Ramón went to the window to look at the garden, he saw, moving about among his choice lettuce heads, something big and strange—nipping, yes, nipping, the young green leaves! He looked and looked, and he thought the strange beast had the shape of a billy goat, yet he was not sure.

"María! María!" he called. "Come, quick, something big and strange is eating up our garden. "Look," he said, pointing to the shape which, having finished with some lettuce, had now turned to some turnips. "Do you see what I see?"

"Ay, Ramón," cried María. "A billy goat came to eat our garden. What shall I do?"

"Do not worry," cried Ramón. "I will go to him and make him go away."

So he went down to the field and patting the billy goat on its back, he said, *"Buenos días, Señor* Billy Goat. Please do not eat up the garden. You are so young and strong and can find food somewhere else, but we are weak and old. Please go away."

But Señor Billy Goat turned and made for him with horns all set.

"Ay, María! María!" cried the old man, running up the hill as fast as he could. "Open the door, please! The billy goat is after me." Puffing and panting, poor Ramón dropped on a chair and began to cry.

"Do not cry," said María. "A little tact is what he needs. I will go to him and make him go away." So she went down to the field.

She tiptoed to where the billy goat was, and bowing low, said, "Buenos días, Señor Billy Goat. That is a fine breakfast you are having. I wonder if you know how long it takes to till the soil, how long to plant the seeds, and how long to pull the weeds. However, I came to ask you . . . ."

That was as far as she got, for the billy goat, tired of her chatter, turned upon her, his legs up in the air and head low for butting the better.

Up the hill went the little old woman, crying, "Ay, Ramón! The billy goat is after me. Open the door, please!" And she, too, tumbled inside the hut.

"*Ay de mí!*" she cried. "Gone are the radishes and the turnips."

"Ruined are the lettuce and the beans," cried the old man.

They cried and cried. Then suddenly something stung Ramón's ears. He shook his head to get rid of it, and as he did so, down dropped a little black ant right into the very palm of his hand.

"*Por Dios*, María, look—la Hormiguita!" he cried.

"I have come to help you," the ant whispered softly. "What will you give me if I do so?"

"How can you help us, Hormiguita?" asked María.

"You are so small, what can you do?" asked Ramón.

"I can make Señor Billy Goat go away," said la Hormiguita.

"You!" cried María.

"Yes, what will you give if I do so?"

"Anything you want," said Ramón.

"Sí, sí, anything," said María.

La Hormiguita thought for a while and then asked for a little sack of flour and one of sugar for her family.

Ramón and María promised, and the little black ant crawled down, and disappeared through a crack in the floor. Out into the open she went, crawling on and on until she reached the field. There was the billy goat, head bent—eating, eating. La Hormiguita crawled up his hind legs and up his back, straight to his ear and stung him.

"Ouch!" cried the billy goat, and he raised one leg to scratch himself. But la Hormiguita had now crawled to the other ear and was stinging him with all its might. "Ouch!" cried the billy goat again, and he raised his other leg to scratch his other ear. But by that time la Hormiguita was crawling up and down his back, stinging as she crawled along.

"Ouch! Ouch! An ant hill! I have stepped on an ant hill," the billy goat cried.

Quickly he jumped out of the vegetable patch

and, thinking that he was all covered with ants, rolled on the ground to shake them off. So he rolled and rolled. Faster and faster he went—rolling . . . rolling . . . rolling, for he forgot he was on a hill, and so he found himself going down, down the hill and out of sight. For all I know, he is still rolling.

But Ramón and María gave la Hormiguita one little sack of flour, and one little sack of sugar, and since then have continued to live happy and contented in their hut.

SENOR COYOTE AND SENOR FOX

In Mexico, there are many stories about Coyote, a character borrowed from the Indians. Coyote is clever—he can get the best of anyone. But once in a while the tables are turned .

Almost everyone in Mexico knows that the Coyote is so smart that he is more or less of a magician. There are very few animals, and no people at all, that can do some of the things that the Coyote can do. And yet, with all his smartness, this smartest of all creatures, *Señor* Coyote, is often made a fool of by creatures smaller than himself. Why this is so would be hard to explain unless it could be said that the Coyote does not think his fellow animals have as much cleverness as they really have.

One day the Coyote was traveling through the country towards a big something that stood up

From *Picture Tales from Mexico,* by Dan Storm. Copyright, 1941, by J. B. Lippincott Company. Published by J. B. Lippincott Company.

on the level plain, like a great cathedral. As he approached it, however, he could see plainly that it was a tall rock cliff more than three hundred feet high. It stood alone, in the middle of the desert.

Señor Coyote arrived at this great cliff and began to walk around it. As he turned the first corner, he noticed some scurrying about at the base of the wall. And whom should he find, but Señor Zorro, little Mr. Fox. The Fox was pushing against the side of the cliff with all his might.

"Aha, my friend Zorro," thought the Coyote. "And so near dinnertime too." Señor Coyote was quite happy with the idea of eating up little Mr. Fox. But the Fox had as quickly schemed a plan of his own.

"Quick!" he shouted. "Help me hold up this cliff! It is falling over and will crush us. *Andale, pronto,* Brother Coyote!"

What the Coyote did not know was something he had not seen. Just as he rounded the first corner, little Mr. Fox had been dozing in the sun. But Señor Zorro never sleeps with both eyes shut. He always has one wide open, looking out for trouble. Half the night he sleeps with one eye open, and half the night with the other open. It is the same for his ears. They both take turns keeping watch while he sleeps. Perhaps this is how Señor Zorro saw the Coyote before Señor Coyote saw him. He had scurried from his sleep in the sun to the side of the wall. And now he was shouting for the Coyote to help, or the cliff would fall.

At first, the Coyote was a bit wary, and thought that the Fox certainly was trying to play some trick on him. So he stood right next to the cliff and looked up toward the top. It did seem that the great tall cliff was slowly toppling over onto him. So, with one spring, he was at the Fox's side, pushing with all his might.

"That was a narrow escape," panted Mr. Fox. "If you hadn't happened along, this rock would have fallen over and crushed me."

The Coyote looked up at the top of the cliff again. And as he did, it seemed to start falling slowly over towards them. Quickly he ducked his head, and began pushing so fast, and with such force, that the gravel flew under his feet.

"This is terrible," said the Fox in a complaining voice. "Perhaps we will have to stay here forever."

"Yes," said the Coyote, "we must stay here until

help comes. If we try to get away from here, the cliff will fall on us before we can run out of danger."

Suddenly the Fox spoke with the cheerfulness of someone who has just thought of a way out of some terrible trouble.

"I know what we can do," he almost sang.

"What, then?" gasped the Coyote, blowing a drop of sweat off the end of his nose.

"I will run for help while you stay here and hold up the cliff," said the Fox, smiling.

"Oh, no," said the Coyote, not too pleasantly. "No, you don't. It takes both of us to hold this thing up. You will stay here, Brother Zorro."

"Why?" said the Fox. "If I held it up for a while by myself, then surely you, with your great strength, can hold it up for the short time it will take me to run and bring help, and chickens and *pulque* and *tortillas.* I will bring others with me and they will be carrying poles to brace this thing up with. Otherwise we will both stay here until we grow into the shape

we are now in, with our hands against the face of this rock. Perhaps our feet will grow roots so deep into the ground that no one can pull us out."

To this the Coyote said nothing, but seemed to be thinking.

"What do you say?" asked the Fox. "How about it, Brother Coyote? I won't be gone more than half an hour."

The Coyote shook his head slowly and then said, "All right then; I guess I am somewhat stronger than I think I am. But do not be gone too long, Brother Zorro."

"Of course not," said the Fox, easing carefully away from the cliff. "*Adiós!* Brother Coyote."

"Remember," said the Coyote pushing harder against the cliff, "half an hour, Brother Fox."

The Fox was gone, lightly loping over the prairie, with a final word called over his shoulder, "Push harder, harder, Brother Coyote. You must make up for both of us, you know."

And so push harder the Coyote did. He pushed until it seemed that his arms would drop off, they ached so badly. It was at these times when his arms were tired that he would steal a quick glance up at the great face of rock extending up to the blue sky, to see if perhaps the cliff had gotten out of the notion of falling.

But no. Every time the Coyote looked up there, the cliff seemed to be starting to topple. So with a quick movement and a grunt or two, the Coyote would dig his feet into the ground and groan and strain and push. And every time he did this, the rocks and dirt would spurt backwards from his churning feet.

A half an hour passed and no Mr. Fox. An hour passed and then two. Mr. Coyote was up to his knees now in a hole he had dug with his feet; and he was calling and singing in his own Coyote voice for Mr. Fox to return. The sun sank below the desert mountains and darkness came. Up came the moon, round and silvery-bright, shining down on Mr. Coyote whimpering, shivering, and yelling for the Fox or for anyone at all.

All night he stood there cursing and suffering, the Coyote did. And imagine, if you can, when daylight came, how there stood the Coyote almost up to his hips in the hole he had dug.

Looking desperately over his shoulder, he said,

"I cannot hold out much longer. I wonder what has happened to the Fox." Up at the cliff he dared not look.

"I will make a break for my life," he said. "I will not last much longer here anyhow. I am about to starve to death."

So, making one last push against the cliff with about all the strength left in his arms, the Coyote leapt out of the hole and without looking up, ran straight out on the plain away from the cliff. As he ran, of course he thought that at any moment the cliff might be on top of him. So fast he went that his legs could not be seen. He looked like some wingless bird flying like the wind close to the ground.

Not until he was at least a half a mile away from the high rock did the Coyote turn and look back, expecting to see the tremendous rock come thundering to earth in a huge cloud of dust. But wonder of wonders, there stood the big rock upright and unchanged. The Coyote could only stare.

"It cannot be," he said. "It is impossible."

Then the truth dawned upon him. The Fox had simply made a fool of him. That was all there was

to it. He was so angry that he jumped up in the
air and came down chasing his tail around and
around while his barks echoed across the desert
to the mountains. And Señor Zorro, where was he?
Quién sabe? (Who knows?)

THE KING OF THE LEAVES

Here again is the wily rabbit. In the United States and the West Indies, he is known as "Br'er Rabbit" or "Brother Rabbit." But in Latin America, he is known as el Conejo (the Rabbit) and Tío Conejo (Uncle Rabbit). In this Nicaraguan tale, the Rabbit is up to his usual tricks.

Tío Conejo—Uncle Rabbit, or Br'er Rabbit, as we call him—has a very bad reputation in Nicaragua. He is famous for being a clever rascal and a shameless rogue. And because he is always making trouble for everybody, the people are tired of him. But he always says he doesn't care what people think or say about him, and he never changes his bad habits.

One day the king of the land said, "We must do something about that troublemaker." The king and his advisers talked it over for a long time, and finally the king said, "Tío Conejo has given us trouble for many years. We must get rid of him. Go out, all of you, and catch him and bring him back to me, dead or alive!"

They all went out, giving suggestions to one another on the best way to catch Tío Conejo.

Finally some said, "Let us go to the water hole, where all the animals come to drink, and hide. Rabbit will get thirsty and come there. Then we'll catch him and take him back to the king. Or maybe if he sees us and is thirsty and can't get any water, he'll go away to another land."

They did not know that Rabbit was right behind the bushes, listening to them talk.

"I will drink all the water I want, and I'll not go away to another land," he said, laughing to himself.

He went to another village and passed by a shoe shop. The shoemaker had beside him a fine pair of shoes for the princess.

"*Buenos días, Señor;* good morning, sir," Rabbit said cheerily to the shoemaker. "It's a hot day."

"It is a very hot day," replied the shoemaker.

"You should sit inside, where it's cool and the

sun won't burn you. At least you should have a drink of cold water. It will do you good."

"That's a good idea," said the shoemaker. "I am thirsty. I'll go into the house and have a drink of cool water from my clay jar."

As soon as he had gone into the house, Tío Conejo took the pretty shoes and away he went—lippety-lop. He came to a highway and followed it—lippety-lop, lippety-lop, lippety-lop.

Far down the road he saw a man coming toward him. The man was walking with his head bent forward and a big gourd on his back.

"Hah! That man is carrying a heavy gourd full of sweet honey. Now, that is something I like," said Rabbit, and he quickly dropped one of the shoes he was carrying in the middle of the road, and hid behind some nearby bushes.

As Rabbit had thought, the man was a honey merchant, and on his back was a big gourd full of sweet, golden honey, which he was carrying to market to sell.

He saw the shoe in the road and stopped. "What a pretty shoe!" he said. "But where is the other one?"

He looked around everywhere, but he could not find the other shoe.

"Well," he said, "one shoe is not worth taking. One must have two to make a pair." So he left the shoe in the road and walked on.

Tío Conejo knew what he was doing. He ran ahead as fast as he could, and when he came to a turn in the road he threw the other shoe down and again hid in the bushes.

Soon the honey man came along and saw the other shoe.

"Ah! There is that other shoe. I'll run back and pick up the first shoe and then I'll have the pair. I'll just put this heavy gourd of honey right here beside the road, behind this bush, where no one will see it, so I won't have to carry it all the way back."

He ran back down the road. As soon as he was gone Tío Conejo jumped out, picked up the gourd, and scampered off with it through the woods. He didn't stop until he came to an open place covered with dead leaves.

There he sat down and ate and ate honey until he was so full he could not swallow another bit. Then he poured the rest of the honey over himself, over his head and long ears, all over his furry body, and over his soft feet and bushy tail. Then he lay down and rolled over and over, until dead leaves stuck to all parts of his body.

Never in this world has anyone ever seen an animal like that. He looked like a great pile of leaves on the move.

Back to the village he went, lippety-lop, lippety-lop. Everybody stared at him. No one had ever seen anything like that before. Many were afraid to come near him.

He went to the water hole where the king's men were waiting to catch him, but no one recognized him. No one came near him.

He put his mouth into the water and drank and drank until he was full and could not drink another drop.

"Who are you?" they asked him.

"I'm the King of the Leaves," he answered, and then he walked away slowly.

This was exactly the way Tío Conejo had said it would be. He came up boldly, drank all the water he wanted, and did not leave the village!

JUAN BOBO

In every country, there are stories about a silly boy. He is always in a muddle, and he turns everything topsy-turvy. In English and American tales, he is "Jack." But in hundreds of Spanish stories, he is "Juan Bobo (silly John). This story is told in Puerto Rico.

There was once a boy so dumb and dull-witted and so stupid that soon people called him Juan Bobo.

He lived with his mother on the hillside of a town. One day his mother sent him to the city to buy meat, molasses, and needles. Juan Bobo saddled his donkey and fixed the baskets lightly. Once in the city, he took his time seeing the sights and enjoying the shop windows. Then he bought the meat, the molasses, and the needles and brought the packages to where the donkey patiently waited. He

unwrapped the meat and put it into one basket. Then he poured the molasses over it. He spread the needles into the other basket, mounted the donkey, and turned towards home.

Now the sun was shining and as he jogged home, the heat of the day began to rise. Flies, attracted by the molasses, buzzed about him and clung to the basket, which was to them like honeycomb.

Poor Juan Bobo! He spent the time wiping his forehead and fighting them. When he finally arrived home, he brought in the meat and gave it to his mother.

"Where are the molasses and the needles?" she asked.

"In the basket, mother," he answered.

But though the mother looked, and looked, she found no trace of either of them, for the molasses had melted and been eaten by the flies and the needles had slipped through the basket.

"Oh, stupid one!" she roared.

When Juan Bobo saw that his mother could not find the molasses, he remembered the flies and how he had struggled to fight them. "Do not fret, mother," he said. "Tomorrow I will go to the judge and denounce the thieves who attacked me on the way and stole my goods."

But his mother ignored his remark. Instead she said, "Go now up the hill and ask my neighbor to lend me her three-legged iron kettle, and do not tarry."

Juan Bobo lost no time in carrying out her wishes, and pretty soon stood at the top of the hill, clutching the iron kettle with the three legs.

Now this was the fork of the road and Juan Bobo sat down to rest. The kettle stood by his side. It was then that he noticed the three legs of the kettle.

"So!" he called, "I have been carrying you. You with three legs and I with only two! It is you who should be carrying me. But I will race you home, that I will." He placed the iron kettle on its three legs on one side of the road and he stood on the other.

"Now," he said, "let us go. One-two-three!"

Down the hill he went at full speed and soon reached home.

"Mother! Mother!" he cried, "did she come? Has she arrived?"

"Who?" asked his mother.

"The iron kettle!" said Juan Bobo. "I raced her

home down the hill."

"The iron kettle!" shouted his mother. "Juan, go get me that kettle, for the fire is lit and I can't wait any longer."

Out of the house like a rocket he shot, and soon was up the hill again. There, in exactly the same place where he had left it, stood the iron kettle, resting on her three legs. Juan lighted on her.

"So, here you stand, you lazy iron kettle. Have you no sense at all? My mother has lit the fire and she can't wait any longer. Are you or aren't you coming home with me?" And he began to kick it with all his force. With one of his kicks he overturned the kettle which, being on an incline, began to roll down the hill.

"Wait! Wait!" he shouted. "I had not yet counted three."

But the kettle rolled straight to Juan's house long before he arrived.

Next day, Juan Bobo, true to his promise, appeared before the judge and explained how he had been accosted on the road by a group of black-veiled ladies who drank up all the molasses he was bringing home to his mother. He demanded their punishment and complete payment of his bill.

"Black-veiled ladies?" asked the judge. "Who are they, and where do they come from?"

He began to laugh, knowing what a simpleton the boy was.

Poor Juan Bobo! He looked around the court and soon discovered two flies alighting upon the tables near by.

"There, your Honor," he said triumphantly. "are two of them now. They must have followed me here."

The judge looked around, expecting to see two persons. Then his eyes followed Juan, who was now taunting the flies with his stick.

The judge pounded his desk with his mallet and laughed until his eyes filled with tears. "Juan Bobo," he called, amid his great laughter, "I cannot make them pay you the bill, but I give you leave to execute the law. Let the weight of your stick fall on them now and wherever you may find them hereafter."

"Yes, your Honor," said Juan Bobo.

At that very moment, he ran to the judge and raising his stick, gave the judge a fierce blow on his head, for three black-veiled ladies had just settled on his bald head.

OVERSMART IS BAD LUCK

The story of "Oversmart Is Bad Luck" is told in many parts of the world. Each country tells, in its own way, about the flattering fox who coaxes the rooster down from his perch. But in Uruguay, the rooster is smarter.

Señor Rooster was a fine bird, and he lived in a village in Uruguay. He was smart, too, and he liked to take walks beyond the village to see the world.

One day he took a long walk and wandered deep into the forest. He came to a tall tree and decided to fly high up into the branches and look at the whole world from there. So he flew up into the tree, branch after branch, until he got high, high up.

Now Señor Fox came walking through the woods. As he passed under the tree he heard Señor Rooster flapping his wings in the branches, and he looked up.

Reprinted by permission of the publisher, The Vanguard Press, from *The King of the Mountains: A Treasury of Latin-American Folk Stories*, by M. A. Jagendorf and R. S. Boggs. Copyright © 1960 by M. A. Jagendorf and R. S. Boggs.

He saw the feathers of Señor Rooster and his fat body, and he thought what a fine dinner he would make. But Señor Fox had no wings and could not fly up into the tree. Nor could he climb. Well, he remembered that good words often pave good roads.

"My dear, dear friend, Señor Rooster!" he cried. "How are you today? I see you are all alone up there. It seems very strange for a famous gentleman like you to be all alone. I'm sure all the fine fat hens in the henhouse are worried about you, wondering where you have gone, and are anxious to see you."

"Good Señor Fox," replied Señor Rooster, "just let them wait. The longer they wait, the happier they will be to see me when I return."

"You're a smart gentleman, Señor Rooster, and very wise. But I wouldn't let the poor hens wait too long. Come down and we'll walk together to the henhouse. I'm going that way."

"Ha, ha, ha!" laughed the rooster. "What sweet and honeyed words you use to catch me! Do you really think I'll come down so you can make a good dinner of me? Sweet words catch fools."

"Don't say that, Señor Rooster. Maybe in my former days of sin I was guilty of such things, but no

more . . . no more . . . I've reformed completely.
Besides, haven't you heard the news? Don't you
know about the new decree now in force in our
forest? No animal can eat another; all are to be
friends. That's the new law. Anyone who breaks it
will be punished severely. I'm surprised you haven't
heard about it. Everyone knows it."

"Well, that's news to me, Señor Fox."

"I wouldn't dare to eat you now, even if I were starving to death, my good friend. Honestly. On my honor."

"Well, it must be so, when you talk like that."

"It's the absolute truth, Señor Rooster. So you see, you can come down now."

"Really!" said Señor Rooster, but still he did not come down. Instead, he looked around in all directions. Suddenly he saw a hunter approaching with his dogs. That gave him an idea. He began to count slowly: "One ... two ... three ... four ...."

"What are you counting, good friend Rooster?"

"Five ... six ...."

"What *are* you counting? Tell me friend."

Señor Rooster pretended he hadn't heard, and said, "Six fine big hunting dogs running this way, and a man with a gun behind them!"

"Dogs! What dogs? Coming this way? With a hunter?"

"Yes, Señor Fox, all coming this way!"

"From which direction are they coming? Please tell me quickly! From where?"

"They're coming from over that way," and he

pointed with his wing in exactly the opposite direction from which he saw them.

"I'd better run along now," cried Señor Fox. "I'm in a hurry." And off he ran, as fast as his legs would carry him.

"Señor Fox! Señor Fox!" called Señor Rooster. "Don't run away! Don't go! You can tell the dogs and the hunter about the new decree among the animals in the forest."

Señor Fox ran into the dogs, and Señor Rooster sat in the tree.

If you dig a pit to catch someone innocent, you often fall into it yourself. Oversmart is bad luck.

THE SACK OF TRUTH

In Europe there are many tales about a "sack of truth." This version is told in Spain.

It makes many years in Spain since there was a king who had only one daughter. Since the *Infanta* was born she had been sickly. Years passed. As she grew older she grew no better; the royal doctors could find no cure for her malady.

"If the doctors of Spain are know-nothings, we will send for those of other countries," said the King.

That brought doctors from everywhere, and only one of them could mention a cure. He was a small Arabian doctor and he said: "Send for the finest pears in Spain. Enough of them will cure her."

So the King ordered pears—baskets of them. Whoever should bring in the best ones and cure the Infanta should have the wish of his heart granted.

The King swore it by the good Santiago, patron saint of all Spain.

Many came bringing good pears and bad pears, yellow and green pears, juicy and withered pears; and the Infanta would eat none of them.

Outside a small village there lived a peasant with three sons. Close to their hut grew a pear tree that every summer was covered with heart-shaped, fragrant pears, the color of gold.

One day the peasant said to the oldest son: "Take a basket, fill it with pears, take it to the King's palace and see can you not cure the Infanta."

The oldest set out with his basket, covered to keep the insects off. On the road he came up with a sad-faced woman carrying a little child. She stopped him and asked: "Boy, where are you going?"

"That isn't your business."

"What does your basket hold?"

"Horns!"

"Then let them be horns!"

Sure enough. When the oldest son reached the palace and uncovered his basket, it was filled with horns. So angry was the King that he ordered him thrown into the dungeon.

After a bit, when the oldest son did not return, the peasant said to the second son: "Something has happened to your brother. Go you, fill a basket with pears and try your luck."

The second son set out. On the road he came up with the sad-faced woman carrying the little child. She stopped him: "Boy, where are you going?"

"That isn't your business."

"What does your basket hold?"

"Stones."

"Then let them be stones!"

Sure enough. When the second son reached the palace and uncovered his basket, it was filled with stones. If the King had been angry before, now he was purple and bursting. He ordered the second son thrown into the dungeon with his brother.

After a bit, when neither son returned, the peasant caught the youngest, whose name was Pedro, filling a basket under the pear tree. He was sad, frightened. "What are you doing? You cannot go. How shall I run the farm with no sons? Why should you be thinking that the youngest will succeed where the oldest has failed?"

The youngest shook his head. No one had ever

thought him very clever, only kind, willing and cheerful. "There is the old saying, you know," he said at last—"'The fingers of one hand are never equal.' I may find luck where my brothers missed it."

So Pedro set out with his basket of pears. On the road he came up with the sad-faced woman carrying a little child. She stopped him and asked: "Boy, where are you going?"

"Mother, I am going to the King's palace."

"What does your basket hold?"

"Pears, to cure the Infanta of her long sickness."

And he thought to himself: "I must not be greedy with those pears. There is the old saying—'He who plays the fox for a day, pays for a year.'" So he uncovered the basket quickly, took out a pear and held it towards the child, saying: "*Nene*, would you like it? It is for you."

The woman took it for the child, smiling, and said: "Then let them be pears to cure! And for the one you have given away, ask what you will in return."

Pedro thought hard. "I would like a whistle which will call to me any animal I choose when I blow it."

"Here it is," said the woman, and she drew out of her kerchief a silver whistle strung on a cord so that Pedro could hang it around his neck.

When he arrived at the palace and uncovered his basket before the King, there were the pears, heart-shaped, fragrant, the color of gold. The King was overcome with joy when he saw them. "They are the best pears in the world!" he cried. "We will take them to the Infanta and see will she eat one."

The Infanta ate one—two—three. She would have eaten them all if the court doctor would have let her. Already there was a faint health showing in her cheeks.

"What do you want?" asked the King.

"My brothers."

The King had them released. Pedro was grateful. He thought of the old saying: 'Gratitude is better scattered than kept in one's pocket.' So he climbed the nearest mountain, blew on his whistle and called to him a wild hare. This he carried to the King. "Mark him, he is yours. Then free him. When I come back I will call him to you again. It shall be a sign between us of two men of honor."

But the King was astonished. "That is beyond your power to call back a wild hare. Nevertheless, if you do it, you shall marry the Infanta."

Over the world went Pedro with his silver whistle; calling to him creatures of all kinds, great and small, fierce and gentle. These he used in good service to others, and you can see how that might be.

At the end of a year he returned to Spain and the King's palace. But while he was still a long way off he blew for the hare and it came running to him, the King's mark still on him. The King saw them approaching from the balcony, the hare under Pedro's arm. He called for his prime minister. "There is that boy back again and with him the wild hare. You must bargain the creature away or I shall have to let him marry the Infanta."

Pedro sold the hare to the minister for a pound of gold. And when he had gone he whistled the hare back to him.

From his balcony the King watched. He saw what had happened. He was frantic-frantic. He called the under-minister. "Go bargain for that hare; and after you have paid for it, see that you don't loose it as the prime minister did. Hurry, hurry."

The under-minister had to pay two pounds of gold for the hare; and before he had reached the palace gates with it, Pedro had whistled it back again.

"This is terrible-terrible!" said the King when he saw what had happened. This time he sent the Infanta, who returned saying that Pedro would only bargain with the King.

So the King went. Pedro drew him into the shadow of a plane tree. "You may have the hare for nothing, Your Majesty, if—you will kiss him."

The King was outraged. But what could he do? "Look carefully about. Is there anyone looking?" he asked.

"No one."

The King kissed the hare. He followed the King back to the palace. Inside, in the Hall of Justice, before the entire court, Pedro asked: "You will keep your promise, yes? I marry the Infanta?"

But the King did not want that. Who ever heard of an Infanta of Spain marrying the son of a peasant? It was abominable. He must think a way out. The prime minister thought of it and whispered in the King's ear: "Tell him he must take a sack, travel the world over and fill it with truth."

The King told Pedro what he must do first if he was to marry the Infanta.

"Good. Fetch me a sack."

The King sent for a large sack.

Pedro took it. He opened the mouth of it until it gaped wide. He said: "I have no need to travel to find truth enough to fill it. King, answer me: Is it not the truth that I brought a basket of the best pears to the palace?"

"It is."

"Truth, go into the sack," and he made a motion as if flinging it inside. "King, is it not the truth that those pears cured the Infanta?"

"It is."

"Truth, go into the sack. King, is it not true that I gave the wild hare to you as a sign between us of two men of honor?"

"It is."

"Truth, go into the sack. King, is it not the truth that you put your mark upon that hare, freed it; and that I brought it back to you again?"

"It is."

"Truth, go into the sack. King, is it not the truth that in order to escape your promise and get the hare from me you kissed . . ."

"Stop!" said the King. "The sack is full of truth."

"And I marry the Infanta?"

"Agreed."

In a day they were married; in a year they had a son; in another year, a daughter. But it took a lifetime for them to get to the end of their happiness.

Glossary

The pronunciation guide is based on Latin American usage. The Spanish *d* is commonly pronounced like the *th* in the English word *then*.

Adiós (ah thee OHS),   good-by

Alcalde (ahl KAHL thay),   mayor

Andale pronto (AHN thah lay PRON toh),   come quickly

Animalita (ah nee mah LEE tah),   dear little animal

Ay (EYE),   oh or say

Ay de mí (EYE thay MEE),   poor me

Belita (bay LEE tah),   Betty

Bobo (BOH boh),   fool

Buenas tardes (BWAY nahs TAHR thehs),   good afternoon

Buenos días (BWAY nohs THEE ahs),   good morning

Carlos (KAHR lohs),   Charles

Conejo (koh NAY hoh),   rabbit

El Escarabajo (ehl ehs kah rah BAH hoh),   The Beetle

Felipa (fay LEE pah),   a girl's name

Infanta (een FAHN tah),   a princess

Juan (hoo AHN),   John

Lagos (LAH gohs),   a make-believe town in Mexico

La Hormiguita (lah ohr mee GHEE tah),   The Little Ant

Mañana(mah NYAH nah),   tomorrow

Manuelito (mah nway LEE toh),   little Manuel

María (mah REE ah),   Maria

Nene (NAY nay),   baby or baby boy

Pastor (pahs TOHR),   shepherd

Pedro (PAY droh),   Peter

Pobrecito (poh bray SEE toh),   poor little one

Por Dios (pohr thee OHS),   for goodness' sake

Pulque (POOL kay,)   a Mexican drink

Quién sabe (kyen SAH bay),   who knows

Ramón (rah MOHN),   Raymond

Ratónperez (rah TOHN pay res),   a storybook mouse

Señor (say NYOHR),   mister

Sí (SEE),   yes

Sombrero (sohm BRAY roh),   hat

Tío (TEE oh),   uncle

Tonto (TOHN toh),   dunce

Tortilla (tohr TEE yah),   a flat cornmeal cake

Zorro (SOH rroh),   fox